WOMEN OF VALOR

The Trials and Triumphs
of Seven Saints

WOMEN OF VALOR

The Trials and Triumphs
of Seven Saints

Alicia von Stamwitz

LIGUORI
PUBLICATIONS

One Liguori Drive
Liguori, Missouri 63057
(314) 464-2500

Imprimi Potest:
John F. Dowd, C.SS.R.
Provincial, St. Louis Province
Redemptorist Fathers

Imprimatur:
+ Edward J. O'Donnell
Vicar General, Archdiocese of St. Louis

ISBN 0-89243-258-6
Library of Congress Catalog Number: 86-82170

Cover design and art by Karen Howe

Table of Contents

Saints Like Us...7

1. **Saint Frances of Rome** 9
   The Radical Housewife

2. **Saint Margaret of Cortona** 17
   The Prodigal Daughter

3. **Blessed Marie Therese de Soubiran**.................24
   Saint of the Mid-Life Crisis

4. **Saint Maria Goretti**..............................33
   The Forgiving Young Woman

5. **Saint Rita of Cascia** 40
   Saint for Spouses of Alcoholics

6. **Blessed Maria Bagnesi** 48
   Saint for the Sick

7. **Saint Hyacintha Mariscotti**........................55
   The Accidental Nun

Saints for Today and Tomorrow 62

Saints Like Us

As a young girl, I kept a book of saints' lives by my bed. Many nights I would read from this marvelous book with the gold lettering on the cover. The stories of heroism and supernatural adventure fascinated me. I dreamed of becoming a saint, chaste and mighty, God's beloved champion.

Then I grew up. I married and became a housewife and mother. I looked at my life one day and felt sad. My dreams of holy adventure now seemed far away, unattainable. Saints do not spend their days changing diapers, running errands, holding down a part-time job, cooking, and cleaning. I picked up a book of saints' lives anyway, hungry for inspiration.

When I stumbled across the life of Saint Frances of Rome I was so surprised I could hardly believe what I was reading. A saint who was a housewife and mother of three? Could this be? A saint with a busy social life, a crotchety mother-in-law, an impulsive and self-willed nature? A saint who decreased her work with the poor so she could spend more time with her children? I read slowly, savoring every ordinary moment of Frances' life. She was my new patron, a model that fit my life.

After discovering Saint Frances of Rome, I spent several months paging through a dictionary of saints' lives. I was determined to unearth more saints who could be models of holiness for women today. I particularly looked for saints who struggled with temptations and problems common to our modern world.

In this book I am happy to present the trials and triumphs of Saint Frances of Rome and six other saints — married, religious, and single. The troubles they faced ranged from selfishness and sexual sins to mental illness, alcoholism in the family, and mid-life crisis. In chronicling each woman's story I have carefully researched her life and times so as to present as authentically as possible her heroism and humanness. I have reported the facts and also mentioned certain popular legends surrounding the saint's life.

A prayer to the saint follows each brief biography. It offers a practical application of the saint's special value for today.

I hope these saints will help other women, as they helped me, to realize their own potential for holiness.

1
Saint Frances of Rome
The Radical Housewife

A twentieth-century Catholic scholar and writer says that we should study the saints because "they make sanctity seem less impossible to us who feel that it would be ridiculous even to try for it."

The lives of many saints, however, seem very different from our own lives. We don't share their religious vocations, their severe penances, or their ability to devote long hours to daily prayer. Instead of feeling encouraged to imitate them, we feel helpless and intimidated by their magnificent stories. "I wish I could be like that" we sigh. "But it's all I can do to keep my marriage together, take care of the house and the kids, and get everyone to Mass on Sunday."

Not every saint, however, is so different from us. Frances of Rome has left a lasting impression not only because of who she was, but because of who she was not. She was a woman and a saint who was not a virgin, not a recluse, and not a martyr in any sense of the word. She was a happily married mother of three with a big house and a busy social life. In this rather ordinary setting, Frances managed to live a radical life of prayer and service to the poor. She is a model for all people who will never wear a habit or live a celibate life or be burned at the stake. She is officially the patron saint of widows, but she could just as well be the patron saint of housewives and mothers.

A loving child

Frances, or Francesa as she would have been known in her homeland, was born in the city of Rome in 1384. Her parents, Paulo and Jacobella Busso, were of noble birth and possessed great wealth. They were ecstatic at the birth of their long-awaited only child. They dressed her in pretty clothes and arranged for her to get a good education: a luxury afforded few women of that century. She was bright and sensitive and eagerly followed her parents in practicing the Christian faith. But Frances was not perfect; she had a strong, sometimes unwieldy self-will.

In 1395, when Frances was eleven, she decided she wanted to be a nun. She asked her parents' permission to enter the convent. Her parents refused for they had already selected a husband for her. Frances was shocked. She tried desperately to persuade them to change their minds. When all attempts failed, she fled to her bedroom determined to run away from home. "Lord," she prayed, "please let something happen to prevent this hateful marriage. . . . You alone have claimed my heart."

Don Antonio di Monte Savello, a Benedictine priest and Frances' spiritual adviser, reproved her later that day. "Do you weep because you want to do God's will," he asked her, "or because you want God to do your will?" He charged her to accept the marriage and suggested it was God's higher calling for her — to grow in holiness amid the distractions of the world.

Loving wife

Frances was barely thirteen when she married Lorenzo Ponziano, the second son of a wealthy and influential Roman family. She moved into her new family's spacious home, struggling to appear relaxed and happy. Frances' greatest concern early in her marriage was that she was not physically attracted to her husband. Don Antonio, her spiritual director, assured her that the success of the marriage was less dependent on her feelings than on the couple's mutual faithfulness, kindness, and forgiveness. Fortunately, Lorenzo was a warm and likable gentleman. Frances felt comfortable in his presence and grew to admire and love him.

At first Frances found her new life difficult. She had many household responsibilities and social obligations. Luckily, she found a close friend in her sister-in-law Vanessa, who shared the same home and, more importantly, the same desire to give herself wholly to God's service. They quickly pledged themselves to daily acts of penance and prayer, and established a secret chapel in an abandoned lookout tower of the grand house. In their free afternoon hours, they brought baskets of food to the city's poor and visited the sick in the nearby Hospital of the Holy Spirit.

Vanessa was the more level-headed of the two. Frances was like Saint Peter — impulsive and given to extremes. Vanessa helped Frances temper her enthusiasms and excesses, encouraging her to maintain her ascetical practices while living outwardly according to the customs of the Ponziano family.

The two women frequently hosted family parties, dressed in stylish gowns of velvet or silk, adorned with gold and precious stones. The more Frances became conscious of her destitute neighbors, the more awkward she felt in her expensive clothing. "Let me put aside these fineries which are the symbols of my wealth," she pleaded with Don Antonio, "and let me clothe myself in such a manner that I may be like the poor."

"Not now," Don Antonio replied. "The time has not yet come. Such singularity now on your part might displease your husband, who does, after all, have a position to keep up."

As it was, there were many in Frances and Vanessa's social circle who criticized the two women harshly. It was not fashionable at that time for noblewomen to take an interest in the poor.

"The unusualness of your actions is drawing ridicule upon our whole family," Frances' mother-in-law, Cecilia, shrilled more than once. When Frances and Vanessa continued to visit the poor, Cecilia spoke to her two sons, demanding they make their wives stop. Lorenzo, however, replied, "My brother and I do not want anyone, not even you, to interfere with the devotions and charitable works of our wives."

Lady of the house

After her mother-in-law died, Frances was chosen to be head of the household. She did not want this overwhelming responsibility and asked that Vanessa be considered instead. Vanessa, for her part, insisted that Frances was better suited for the position, and Vanessa prevailed.

Frances quickly went about improving the servants' living quarters, spelling out her expectations of them, and arranging their hours of employment so that all who wished might attend daily prayers and Mass. She was demanding but fair, treating the servants as younger brothers and sisters.

Shortly after Frances took over the management of the household, the city of Rome endured a serious flood followed by sickness and famine. Frances and Vanessa doubled their efforts to bring relief to the poor. Frances ordered the household servants not to refuse help to anyone who came to their door. As the word of this generosity spread, the poor came in droves.

When Frances' father-in-law saw how recklessly she distributed his carefully stocked provisions, he was furious and took the key to the storeroom from her. But Frances was not discouraged. Legend has it that she prayed over an empty corn bin and it was inexplicably replenished, as was an empty wine barrel. Seeing this miracle, Andrew Ponziano was sick with remorse. He returned the key to Frances and asked her to pray for him, that he might learn to be more generous.

Devoted mother

Frances and Lorenzo had been married for five years and had suffered the death of three infants shortly after birth before Frances bore a healthy boy whom they named John Baptist. Two more healthy children followed: another boy, Evangelist, and a girl, Agnes. Frances chose not to entrust her children to a nursemaid, as was the custom for women in her position. Instead, she spent fewer hours caring for the poor and devoted more time to her children.

Tragically, Evangelist died when he was nine. A year after his death, Frances had one of her most dramatic spiritual experiences. It is said that Evangelist appeared to her during her evening hour of prayer. She stared at him, thinking him a dream. Then Evangelist spoke to her, describing the splendors of heaven and the nine choirs of angels that surround the throne of God, crying "Holy, Holy, Holy Lord, God of Hosts." He told Frances that he had been sent to warn her of Agnes' impending death and to tell her that God would give her a special consolation — an archangel to guide her for the remainder of her life.

Agnes became sick shortly after this vision and died at the age of sixteen. The promised archangel became visible to Frances from this time on, but to no one else. Frances tried to describe her dazzling companion to Don Antonio, even attempting to put the angel's hand in his, but the grasp was as air to the priest.

To Frances, the angel was a model of goodness and a mirror who reflected her inner thoughts. The angel's presence increased her desire to please God. The angel counseled her, at one point commanding her to stop performing her severe penances (subsisting on bread and water and wearing a painful hair shirt). "You should understand by now," the angel said, "that the God who made your body and gave it to your soul as its servant never intended that the spirit should ruin the flesh and returned it to him despoiled."

Angel of mercy

Civil wars, famines, and epidemics ravaged Rome. Frances turned a large hall of the house into a makeshift hospital and kept a huge pot of soup warming over a fire in the kitchen. When the household provisions were exhausted, Frances and Vanessa begged for food, both for their family and for the poor who continued to flock to the Ponziano home.

In the winter, the two women made daily trips to the outskirts of the city, gathering branches and dead vines and loading them on a donkey. They distributed the firewood among the poor in the slums, to warm the tumbledown shacks that made such pitiful shelters against the cold. When one of the more serious epidemics swept through Rome, Frances drove a wagon up and down the streets, collecting the bodies that lay on the sides of the road and preparing them for burial.

In caring for the sick and wounded, Frances applied home-made herbal ointments to her patient's sores to soothe and help them heal. Then she placed her hands on the sick person and prayed. It soon became apparent that Frances was gifted with special healing powers: At times the cures that followed her ministrations were instantaneous and miraculous. Frances tried to hide this grace, but word of these healings spread quickly and she was overwhelmed with desperate requests. There are two especially popular stories of her healing power.

On one occasion, Frances and Vanessa found a frail, elderly man half-dead in the streets. His arm had been severed by a soldier's saber, and he was lying in a pool of blood. The two women carried the man home on a stretcher. Vanessa whispered to Frances, "We will have to bury his poor arm first thing in the morning." Frances did not answer, but anointed the severed stump and shoulder with her homemade salve. The man's flesh instantly closed over the wound, reuniting arm to shoulder. The man sprang out of bed and ran up and down the halls, flexing his muscles like a schoolboy and shouting the good news.

Another time, a woman came screaming and weeping to Frances, clutching the lifeless body of her infant son. The mother was especially distressed because she had not had the child baptized. Frances took the small child in her arms and held the body tightly to her breast. Then she prayed, made the Sign of the Cross on the baby's forehead, and kissed his cold lips. When she handed the baby back to its mother his eyelids fluttered and he began to whimper. Frances urged the astounded mother to have the baby baptized at once.

Oblates of Mary

In 1425 Frances felt free to carry out a project that had been on her mind for some time. She wanted very much to found a new kind of religious community, one that would offer the challenges and support of religious life to women who were unable to enter the convent. A small group of Roman noblewomen who had followed Frances' example formed the basis of the unique community, the Oblates of Mary. They lived in their own homes, but were bound together under the direction of the Benedictines in prayer and service to the poor.

Though the new community depended greatly on Frances for its growth and direction, she knew that her first duty was to her husband. Lorenzo especially needed her love and support in his last years. She stayed by his side throughout his long, final illness. Over the years they had come to love one another deeply, and his dying words must have comforted her long after his death: "I feel . . . oh, I feel as if my whole life has been one beautiful dream of purest happiness. God has given me so much in your love."

Frances was 52 when Lorenzo died. A few years earlier, the Oblates of Mary had purchased a house for the widowed and single members of the group. Frances moved into the house, and was quickly appointed the superior.

Certain townspeople complained that Frances' oblates were odd, neither secular nor religious in the traditional sense.

When Frances requested official approbation for her community, however, Pope Eugenius IV gladly sent his blessing and more. "I recommend myself and my work to the saint," were his prophetic words, "and I beg you to ask her for her prayers."

Her death

Frances died in the spring of 1440, at the age of 56. "The heavens open and the angels are coming to meet me," she said. "They beckon me to follow them." A perfume like a blend of spices and lilac blossoms filled the house.

During Frances' wake, miracles followed miracles in rapid succession. Huge crowds pressed around the house hoping to touch or to see Frances. Frances' family grew concerned over the intensity of the excited mob and decided to speed her burial. The crowds would not allow it. The burial was delayed till all who wished to pay their respects had visited the bier of the beloved saint.

Frances was canonized in 1608 by Pope Paul V. Her feast is celebrated on March 9.

> *Dear Frances,*
> *I want the courage*
> *to give more than a sandwich*
> *or a dollar*
> *to a poor person.*
> *But I am afraid.*
> *What if I am taken advantage of,*
> *or scorned and mocked?*
> *What if I become too involved*
> *and am dragged down?*
> *Please help me to have the courage*
> *to truly care about one poor person.*

2
Saint Margaret of Cortona
The Prodigal Daughter

God is always standing us on our heads. Just when we think we've got things figured out, he does something unexpected and wonderful. Take the story of the Prodigal Son, for instance. The bad guy wins. The good, obedient son receives no reward. It's not fair. Depending on whose side we take in the story, it makes us either mad or very, very happy.

The story of Margaret of Cortona is a paradox too. Like the Prodigal Son, she sinned recklessly for many years until she realized her own wretchedness. She stumbled back to God not only to be received by him but to be saturated with his love and made into a saint.

Early life

Margaret was born in Laviano, a little town in rural Italy, in the year 1247. An only child, her parents adored her and gave her every comfort a farmer's income could afford.

When Margaret was only seven, her mother died. As her father was busy with the farm, the beautiful little girl was often left to herself. Margaret was lonely and starved for affection.

When her father remarried two years later, things grew worse instead of better. Her stepmother was a hard and impatient woman who resented young Margaret. She treated her nine-year-old stepdaughter cruelly, making Margaret more miserable than ever.

As she entered her teens, Margaret was definitely a "head-turner." She enjoyed the stares and compliments of the young men of Laviano. She eventually yielded to their advances, so hungry was she for the attention and love denied her at home. By the time she was eighteen, Margaret had earned quite a reputation in her hometown.

Occasionally a certain nobleman from Montepulciano would ride through Laviano. He, too, noticed Margaret. It wasn't long before she became his lover. He persuaded the young woman to elope with him and live in his castle, promising her marriage and riches. Life in the castle was certainly luxurious, but Margaret's lover never fulfilled his promise to marry her.

For nine years Margaret lived openly as mistress to this young nobleman, bearing him a son. She would often be seen riding through Montepulciano on a majestic, well-trained horse, her silks and velvets tossing in the wind, her jewels sparkling in the bright sunlight. The townspeople were scandalized by this proud, immoral stranger and her openly sinful lifestyle.

Heading home

The turning point in Margaret's life came suddenly. Her lover went away on business and did not return at the appointed time. Margaret became anxious. She sent a servant out to look for him, then sat by a window watching the roads and paths leading to the castle. As she watched, she was startled to see her lover's favorite dog scratching at the locked castle gate.

As soon as the gate was opened, the dog ran to Margaret and began to whine and tug at her dress. She followed him to a heap of wood in the forest, where he began to whine more loudly and poke at the wood. Margaret, trembling, pulled off the top sticks and uncovered the bruised head of her lover. She screamed and fell to the ground, unconscious.

The murder struck Margaret like a bolt from heaven. She interpreted it as God's judgment against her and was filled with shame and sorrow for her sins. She returned to the castle and gave away all of her possessions. Then, pulling on a plain robe, she took her little son by the hand and headed back to her father's house.

Like the father of the Prodigal Son, Margaret's father was ready to forgive her and welcome his daughter and grandson into his home. Her stepmother, on the other hand, raised such a protest that her father was forced to send Margaret and her son away.

Margaret despaired as she walked away from her father's house. Her little son was crying from hunger and exhaustion. She stopped in a garden and sat under a fig tree, struggling to hold back her own tears as she comforted her son. She considered returning to the castle, but her conscience protested. "No, no, Margaret. Don't live in shame and remorse anymore. To beg for your food would be better than to go back to that place of sin." She encouraged her son and they started out on the twelve-mile walk to the city of Cortona.

The call of Saint Francis

At the city gate of Cortona, two wealthy ladies noticed the pretty young stranger with her tired little boy. They had pity on Margaret and took her and the boy into their home.

Margaret told them about her past life and her desire to lead a life of penance under the guidance of the Friars Minor in Cortona. The ladies were themselves devoted to Saint Francis and his Order and promised to help her. They brought her to the Franciscan church and introduced her to Father Giunta Bevegnati. He agreed to be her confessor but thought it best to test her vocation before clothing her in the habit of the Third Order.

Margaret remained in the house of her two kind friends, supporting herself and her son by serving as midwife and nurse for the wealthy women of Cortona. She attended Mass daily, befriended and cared for the poor, and spent long hours in prayer. After three years, Father Giunta was ready to admit her to the Third Order.

At this time, Margaret decided to send her son to a school in Arezzo where he would be educated by the Friars Minor. He later joined the Order, becoming a Franciscan priest.

Mother of sinners

Now Margaret was ready to live the life of a penitent without any reservations. She moved into a small cottage in a secluded area and gave up her work as nurse and midwife. She spent most of her time in prayer and contemplation. Any time that remained she spent helping the poor and teaching the Gospel to the people who came to visit her.

As her prayer life advanced, Margaret is said to have experienced ecstasies and visions. In times of prayer, it was as if the Lord spoke plainly to her. For a long time he called her "My poor little one." Then one day, he called her "My daughter." Margaret was intoxicated with joy: "My daughter! My daughter!" she sang. "My Lord has called me, 'My daughter!' "

Many were converted by Margaret's teaching and example. People flocked to Cortona from other cities to see and hear the reformed mistress. "I have made you the mother of sinners," the Lord said to Margaret. "I call to them but they are deaf to my voice. You are a mirror for sinners, an example that I offer to them. You are a net to catch sinners, a source of confidence for those who despair."

At one point, Father Giunta, who heard the confessions of her converts, complained to Margaret about the ever-increasing number of people she was sending to him. When Margaret relayed his complaint to the Lord, he answered, "Margaret, your confessor has told you that he cannot clean so many stables in one day. Tell him that in hearing confessions he does not clean stables, but that he prepares a dwelling place for me."

In her eagerness to please God, Margaret devised ways to humiliate herself and deface her body. She made a plan to go to Montepulciano dressed in rags with a rope around her neck and to have a hired woman lead her through the streets calling out: "Here is that proud and haughty woman whom you used to see clothed in silk and gold! Now treat this wretched woman who was the shame of your city as she deserves!" Father Giunta put a stop to her plans. "It would be unseemly in a young woman and could be viewed as spiritual pride instead of true mortification," he said. He suggested she go instead to the church in Montepulciano one Sunday and ask pardon of the congregation.

Another time she planned to cut and scar her face, whose beauty still drew many stares. Again her confessor stopped her. Finally, she asked God to take away from her any grace and beauty that might make people admire her. The loving Father declined her request and answered, "By your beauty I wish to encourage sinners to come to you, be converted, and thus contribute to my glory."

Madwoman of Cortona

Margaret soon discovered that she did not need to look for humiliation: Humiliation and trials would find her. From the beginning there were people in Cortona who doubted Margaret's sincerity. After she joined the Third Order of St. Francis they began spreading rumors about her, accusing her of having relations with Father Giunta. The townspeople began calling her "madwoman" and treating her with contempt. When the rumors did not stop and suspicions grew, even the Friars began to doubt Margaret's virtue and holiness. To quiet the rumors, they were eventually forced to transfer Father Giunta to Siena. He did not return to Cortona until shortly before Margaret's death.

After this episode of suspicion, Margaret began the long journey through her spiritual desert. God did not communicate with her and she lost all sense of his presence and love. When at last he returned, Margaret cried out: "Lord, why did you abandon me for so long?"

"I did not abandon you," the Lord answered. "I always remain near you. But you cannot hope to nourish yourself continually on the milk of sensible consolations. Know that your faithfulness in times of dryness and in the absence of interior consolations honors me more and is more profitable for you, because then you serve me not according to your own choice but according to mine."

Margaret was repeatedly tempted to scrupulosity and tormented by Satan. He tried to terrify her with horrible visions and accusations. He told Margaret that her sins were too many and too great for her to obtain God's forgiveness. He said that eventually God would abandon her and her damnation would then be final.

To his frightened child, the Lord said, "If Lucifer could break out of hell and join your enemies to deceive you, he would, so furious is he against you, due to the state of grace to which I have raised you. But you shall be well protected, my daughter, for I will always be with you."

The last years

The way became easier for Margaret after she had endured these trials. When she was almost forty, the Lord told her that she could now leave the city of Cortona and spend the rest of her life in private prayer and seclusion. She was not left alone for very long, however. The people of Cortona (who by now had seen the error of their evil rumors) as well as citizens from Siena, Florence, and even from Rome came to her seeking advice and prayers. The sick and troubled came to Margaret with their concerns. They left her presence feeling strengthened and renewed. She had a special gift for reading hearts and gently reminded sinners of their faults and the importance of making a good confession.

Margaret died on February 22, 1297, at the age of fifty. She had known the date of her death for a month and had been awaiting it peacefully. On the morning of her death, she said to her friends, "The way of salvation is easy; it is enough just to love."

Margaret of Cortona was canonized by Pope Benedict XIII in 1728. Her feast is celebrated in a special way by the Franciscan Order and the Diocese of Cortona.

Dear Margaret,
Some days I think I am a good person.
Other days I feel so sinful and wretched
I want to hide.
You did not hide.
You faced your sins
and confessed them to others.
With bold faith
you asked God to have mercy on you.
Please pray for me.
I want to believe
that God can love me
as much as he loved you.

3
Blessed Marie Therese de Soubiran
Saint of the Mid-Life Crisis

How would you like your biography to be called *A Study in Failure*? This is the actual title of a biography of Blessed Marie Therese de Soubiran written shortly after her death.

Most saints' lives boast of miracles, spiritual triumphs, and personal achievements. The story of Marie Therese is different. It is a story of frustrated dreams and loneliness. At the untender age of thirty-nine, Marie Therese had to begin her life over. In one year she was excluded from her religious community, lost contact with her dearest friends, and suffered the loss of her job and her reputation.

No one would choose a life like Marie Therese's. But if you are called to share some part of her difficult journey, she will encourage you to hold your head high and to walk on with grace and dignity.

Early life

Marie Therese was born in 1835 in Castelnaudary, France. She was the second child born to Joseph and Noemie de

Soubiran, a Catholic couple of royal ancestry. Marie Therese's older brother died in infancy, as did three of the four children who followed. Only one sister, born when Marie Therese was six years old, survived to become her playmate and companion.

Marie Therese was quiet and reserved. She was educated at home by her uncle, Father Louis de Soubiran, a strict and zealous teacher. When she was ten, Father de Soubiran was put in charge of the Castelnaudary Sodality of Our Lady. The sodality had started as a Catholic girls' club with the simple aim of keeping young girls off the streets. Father de Soubiran turned it into a serious group of lay apostles. He brought Marie Therese to a position of responsibility in the sodality and groomed her for religious life.

For the next eight years Father de Soubiran quietly proceeded to set the stage for the foundation of a "Beguinage." Beguinages were a type of Christian community that had thrived in France in the Middle Ages. As a compromise between religious and secular life, members wore habits and worshiped together but did not necessarily live together or take vows of poverty, chastity, or obedience.

After buying land and a group of cottages, Father de Soubiran announced his plan to revive the Beguinage. He asked eighteen-year-old Marie Therese to be the community's first superior.

At first Marie Therese said no. She had been considering the cloistered life of a Carmelite. The Beguinage would be a step away from this dream. Father de Soubiran persisted, and her spiritual director also voted for the Beguinage. A year later, Marie Therese agreed to give the community a try. She professed her first commitment to the group at the age of nineteen, along with five other sodality friends.

Within two years there was a steady flow of postulants to the Beguinage. The women taught poor children and began welcoming homeless orphans into their cottages. More beds were needed, and then more space. Marie Therese built a new convent and orphanage.

Foundress

The new community was succeeding, but Marie Therese was not at peace. As the years passed she felt increasingly uneasy living the life of a beguine. She was not alone in this feeling. One by one the women came to her, expressing their desire to lead the life of a vowed religious. Marie Therese's younger sister, who had followed her into the Beguinage, was among those eager for a deeper commitment.

Marie Therese was faced with two choices. She could release the restless women, letting them move on to different Orders, or she could alter the character of the Beguinage to give the women a full religious rule.

After praying and thinking it over for a year, Marie Therese decided to establish a new congregation. The Congregation of Our Lady Help of Christians was founded in 1864. Convents were established in Castelnaudary and in the newly industrialized city of Toulouse.

At Toulouse the nuns continued to care for orphans and to teach poor children. They also adopted some new ministries. Marie Therese was quick to notice the unique problems of the city's young female factory workers. Having left families behind when they took jobs in the city, the girls were often alone and afraid. Their jobs paid poorly and they could not afford decent housing or nutritious food.

Within a year the Congregation of Our Lady Help of Christians had opened a hostel for working girls, the first of its kind. It was called simply, "Family House." For a reasonable rate, working girls received a comfortable room and good meals. Marie Therese did not stop with meeting the girl's physical necessities. She found ways to create a warm and caring atmosphere in the home.

If a girl had to work late, Marie Therese sent a nun to meet her at the end of the shift. She was walked safely home. Regardless of the hour, a hot meal was waiting for her when she got in. Marie Therese furnished a game room and organized parties for the girls. A choir was formed. Continuing education classes were started.

Needless to say, the factory girls loved their home. After three years, eight hundred girls were either living in the house or regularly joining in its activities.

As the Congregation of Our Lady Help of Christians flourished, the pace of Marie's life quickened. Postulants flowed in. A convent and novitiate opened at Borges. Family Houses were opened in Amiens and Lyons, then two more convents and orphanages in other cities. By 1873, the community was a dream come true. No one would have guessed that Marie Therese was about to enter her life's nightmare.

Sister Marie Francoise

Sister Marie Francoise Borgia had entered the Congregation in 1868 as a postulant. She was an intelligent, zealous woman who had published two books on the spiritual life. She was also Marie Therese's senior by five years. She came to the order with radiant recommendations from several priests. Attractive and capable, Marie Francoise Borgia won over the Sisters immediately.

Marie Therese was as impressed as anyone. She took the new postulant with her as a traveling companion when she went to Rome to ask for papal approbation of the Congregation. Then she took her to Amiens and Lyons to oversee new projects. Marie Francoise Borgia made her first profession in 1870 at the age of forty-one. A short while later, Marie Therese made Marie Francoise her top assistant.

Marie Francoise went about her work with admirable enthusiasm. She created new projects one after another and campaigned tirelessly for community support of her ideas. In Marie Therese's words, she captivated the nuns with "the brilliance of her explanations, the force and clarity of her arguments, the justness of her estimates, her shrewdness, tact, and skill in affairs . . . and the lively and warm faith that animated her."

Then, in February of 1874, Marie Francoise Borgia made a shocking announcement: The community was on the verge of bankruptcy. There was a frightening debt of a million-and-a-half francs. Speaking to the bewildered councillors, Marie Francoise blamed the Congregation's financial crisis on mismanagement. She suggested that the foundress be removed from her administrative position.

Marie Therese was stunned. Of course there were considerable debts for buildings and land, but as far as she knew, the debts were being steadily paid off. However, Marie Therese trusted her assistant's judgment. Marie Francoise was well-respected and had consistently proven herself to be a shrewd businesswoman. Marie Therese did not have the confidence or resources to contradict her assistant.

The council panicked. Marie Francoise coolly assured the nuns that with a capable person in authority, the community might yet be saved from utter ruin. The council begged Marie Francoise to take the lead.

It did not occur to anyone to verify Marie Francoise's alarming story.

Dismissal

With everyone doubting her, Marie Therese had trouble defending herself and explaining the debts. She sought the advice of her spiritual director, Father Paul Ginhac. Father Ginhac summoned Marie Francoise Borgia, that he might hear the other side of the story. As always, Marie Francoise captivated her listener with her animated, articulate speech. Father Ginhac urged Marie Therese to resign. The Archbishop of Bourges accepted the resignation and appointed Marie Francoise as the new superior.

Once Marie Francoise was in control, she suggested to the Bishop that it would be better if Marie Therese were away for a short time while the community was getting reorganized. Marie Therese found shelter with the Sisters of Charity at Clermont. During her seven-month exile, Marie Therese wrote forty-one letters to her new superior asking for clarification of her status in the community. To Marie Therese, Marie Francoise said that the council did not want her back. To the council, Marie Francoise said that Marie Therese had abandoned the community. A short while later, Marie Therese was officially dismissed from the Congregation of Our Lady Help of Christians.

As if losing her religious community and her position of leadership were not enough, Marie Therese was also denied the solace of her sister and her dearest friend. Marie Francoise decreed that no one in the Congregation, not even Marie Therese's sister, should have contact by letter or in person with the former foundress. Stripped of honor and alone in the world, Marie Therese wrote in her journal, "God only knows my suffering and anguish. It is difficult not to be allowed to devote myself, to have nobody's trust, to be unable to unburden my heart."

Starting over

It would be easy at this point to second-guess the judgment and actions of Marie Therese. "She should have known about her assistant." "She could have fought harder to remain within her community." "If only she had done this or that, the whole thing could have been prevented."

It is quite possible that Marie Therese spent many lonely hours turning these questions over in her mind. Her great achievement was to leave these questions unanswered and to begin anew. It is a remarkable example of detachment. She did not cling to the community she had borne and nurtured. She placed it in God's hands and bravely walked away to look for a different order.

First she approached the Visitation nuns. Of course, word had gotten around that the foundress' own Congregation did not want her. She was regarded with suspicion. After several days of discussion, the Visitation nuns refused to accept her into their community. Marie Therese knocked at the door of the Carmelite convent and was again rejected.

But Marie Therese was determined. A third time she knocked, and the door was opened — a crack. The Order of Our Lady of Charity in Toulouse accepted her not as a postulant, but as a temporary boarder. The one-time administrator of a flourishing community was now in charge of darning stockings.

Marie Therese did her job cheerfully, glad to be busy at any task after her demoralizing ordeal. In time she was accepted as a postulant. At age forty-two, Marie Therese made her second religious profession. She joined in the community's challenging apostolate — to shelter and rehabilitate prostitutes. Her last twelve years were spent in this Order.

Marie Therese died on June 7, 1889, at the age of fifty-four. She had been confined to the infirmary with tuberculosis since the previous winter. She said to her Sisters, "It is happiness for me. Please God it won't distress you, but I do want to go to God."

Honor restored

Shortly after Marie Therese's death, Marie Francoise resigned from her office as superior of the Congregation of Our Lady Help of Christians. Her instability and thirst for power had finally been recognized by the Sisters. They voted down her proposals and refused to ratify arbitrary changes. When Marie Francoise saw that she would no longer get her way she stomped out of the community, never to be seen again.

After her death in 1921, it was learned that Marie Francoise was a married woman when she joined the community. She had deserted her husband, an epileptic, after four years of marriage. As her husband was still alive when she made her profession, Marie Francoise was never validly a nun.

As for the financial crisis of 1874, it was a gross exaggeration of a manageable problem. She had lied to the council to gain the seat of power.

It is a sad story, but one with a redemptive ending. After Marie Francoise resigned, the new Superior worked hard to restore the Congregation in the spirit of Marie Therese. Within a short time the Congregation of Our Lady Help of Christians was once again a stable and honorable treasure of the Church. Marie Therese's cause for canonization was introduced, and in 1946 she was beatified. Her feast is celebrated on October 20.

Model for us

Marie Therese is a model for anyone who has suffered a great wrong or loss. Though her suffering was intense, she did not give in to bitterness, cynicism, or self-pity. She clung to her hope in God, believed that right would triumph, and marched forward to a meaningful new life. Her spirit lives on in her own words:

As you may imagine, all this did not happen without extreme suffering. Only God can measure its depth and intensity. Only he knows the grace of faith, hope and love that flow from it. The great truth that God is all, and the rest nothing, becomes the life of the soul. Upon it one can lean securely amid the incomprehensible mysteries of this world. This is a good above all other good on earth, for it is on almighty love that we rely for time and eternity. Should I have learned this without such cruel anguish? I do not think so. Time passes, and it passes quickly. We shall soon know the reason of so many things that surprise and shock our feeble, shortsighted reason.

Dear Marie Therese,
Why me? throbs in my head
day after day.
I do not want to be who I am
where I am.
Pain and sorrow sap my strength.
Please pray for me, Marie Therese.
Help me open my eyes
to what can still be.
Give me the wisdom and hope to say
Who can I become now?
Where can I go tomorrow?

4
Saint Maria Goretti
The Forgiving Young Woman

JULY 5, 1902

It is Saturday, early afternoon. A twelve-year-old girl with chestnut hair sits on the porch of a small two-family house. She is mending a shirt. On a quilt beside her, a baby sleeps.

Not far from the house their mother is threshing dry beans. Four other children are with the mother, merrily riding an oxcart around the threshing floor. The family's neighbors work nearby: a widower and his nineteen-year-old son.

Before long the neighbor's son excuses himself and walks toward the house. He steps past the girl on the porch, entering the kitchen. He goes to his room and emerges with a long, newly sharpened knife. He places the knife on a counter in the kitchen. Then he calls to the girl sitting on the porch.

"What do you want?" she asks, frightened.

"I tell you to come inside," he repeats.

"No," she answers. "I won't unless you tell me what you want."

The young man trembles with impatience. He runs out to the porch. In one swift motion he grabs the girl by the arm and drags her into the kitchen, locking the door behind him.

"What are you doing?" the girl shrieks as he yanks at her dress. "No! No! Do not touch me. It is a sin! You will go to hell!" With incredible strength, she struggles with the young man.

The young man is enraged. He grabs the knife and stabs the girl thirteen times, quickly silencing her screams. She falls to the floor and is still. The young man turns and begins to walk away.

The girl stirs. "My God, my God!" she moans. "I am dying. Mamma! Oh, Mamma!" The young man wheels around and stabs the girl again.

The baby, alone on the porch, awakens and begins to cry. Her loud, frightened cry finally pierces the noise of the threshing.

This, in a nutshell, is the story of Saint Maria Goretti, a young girl from Ferriere de Conca in southern Italy who resisted rape, accepting death as the consequence.

The story does not end here. This is more than a story of attempted rape and murder. It is also a story of compassion, conversion, and reconciliation. Maria Goretti, her mother, and her murderer each have heroic stories to tell.

Maria

Maria was still alive when her mother, Assunta, rushed to answer the baby's frightened cry and found Maria lying on the kitchen floor. Maria was immediately taken to the hospital.

For two excruciating hours, a team of doctors worked to save the young girl. They were hours of severe suffering for Maria, since in her condition it was impossible for the doctors to give her an anesthetic. The knife had passed through her lungs and intestines and pierced her heart. After providing all the relief they could, the doctors made Maria as comfortable as possible, knowing that it was just a matter of time before she would die.

That night, the process of dehydration under way, Maria's throat became parched, her tongue swollen. She burned with fever and a vicious thirst. "Water, please," she whispered. But the doctors had forbidden it. "Can't you even give me just one little drop of water, Mamma?" she pleaded. Assunta, in pain at seeing her daughter's suffering, could only shake her head and say no.

Delirious from the fever, Maria twice relived her terrifying encounter with Alessandro.

"What are you doing?" she cried out wildly. "No, Alessandro! No! Do not touch me!"

The next morning, drifting in and out of consciousness, Maria spoke with Father Signori. He had given Maria her First Communion just months before. He was now to give Maria her last Communion.

"Maria," the priest asked gently as he prepared to give her the host, "do you remember how Jesus forgave his executioners when he was dying on the cross? Remember how he told the penitent thief, 'Today you will be with me in paradise'?"

"Yes," Maria answered.

"Can you, Maria, forgive your murderer with all your heart?"

"Yes," she said. "I too, for the love of Jesus, forgive him. And I want him to be with me in paradise. May God forgive him, because I have already forgiven him."

At three o'clock that afternoon, Sunday, July 6, Maria Goretti died. Her holiness was evident not only in her desire to preserve her chastity but also in her unhesitating, total forgiveness of her murderer. At a time when anger would have been normal and expected, Maria showed astonishing compassion. Wracked with pain, denied water, denied life, she said, "Poor Alessandro. How unfortunate you are. I forgive you. I want you to be with me in paradise."

Alessandro was later to discover the power in Maria's words.

Alessandro

Maria had told her mother as they waited for the ambulance that it was Alessandro who had assaulted her. As soon as the ambulance drove off, a crowd of neighbors began to look for her young assailant. They beat on his locked bedroom door, but there was no sound from inside. A robust, middle-aged woman lost her patience and gave the door an angry kick. The door swung open. Alessandro was found lying on his bed face-down, as if sleeping.

The neighbors would have pounced on the young man and killed him if it were not for the arrival of the police. They drove the people back and called for reinforcements to protect Alessandro from the growing mob. He was taken to police headquarters amid a volley of stones, howls, and threats.

At his trial on October 16, the birthday of Maria Goretti, Alessandro was cynical and unrepentant. When asked why he had killed Maria, he replied, "I have a headache."

His lawyer pleaded insanity. "Nonsense," said the court psychiatrists who had examined him. "We judge Alessandro Serenelli fully responsible for the crime he has committed."

Alessandro was declared guilty and sentenced to thirty years' imprisonment with hard labor. To assure his safety and avoid a confrontation with the agitated townspeople, he was moved in the middle of the night to a penitentiary in Noto, Sicily, to serve his term.

Prison life was difficult, but Alessandro was hard to break. For years he retained his sullen, remorseless stance.

Then one night Alessandro had a dream. He found himself in a garden filled with exotic, fragrant flowers. Scores of lilies, more white and beautiful than he had ever seen, filled the wonderful garden. Then he saw a girl with flowing, dark hair. She bent over the lilies and began gathering them, twining them into a garland. His throat tightened and he tried to cry out. The girl turned, and he shrank back. When he looked more closely, he saw that her eyes were soft. She smiled at him and drew closer. "Maria! Oh, Maria!" he cried helplessly. Her arms overflowed with lilies and she extended them toward him.

"Take them," she said gently. He took the lilies in his trembling arms and watched, transfixed, as one by one the lilies became bright, glowing flames. When he awakened from his dream, Maria and the lilies were gone but the memory remained.

From that night on, Alessandro changed noticeably. He wrote to the bishop of the Diocese of Noto. "I am deeply sorry for depriving an innocent person of life, one who, to the very end, was intent on safeguarding her honor, sacrificing her life rather than yielding to my sinful desires. I wish to make public my detestation of my crime and ask pardon of God and the distressed family of my victim."

Alessandro was freed after twenty-seven years in prison, three years of his sentence waived for good conduct. He first got a job breaking stones, then found employment as a farmer. When fellow-workers asked who he was and where he came from, he did not answer directly. He quietly replied that he had committed a very great crime in his youth for which he was deeply sorry. "I am the repentant thief," he said to one worker, no doubt having heard of Maria's dying wish that he might join her in paradise.

Soon after he had been released, Alessandro was sought out and cautiously asked if he would testify in the process for Maria's beatification. He quickly agreed. "It is my duty!" he said. "I must make reparation and I must do all in my power to glorify Maria. She was truly a saint." He then added, "I hope I may yet be saved, because I have a saint in heaven praying for me."

Only one thing remained to be done. Alessandro wrote to Assunta, Maria's mother.

Assunta

Imagine how Assunta felt when she received word that Alessandro wished to see her. This was the man who had killed her Maria. This was the person who had made it necessary for her to entrust her two remaining little girls to the care of others. With her husband and her eldest daughter dead, Assunta had no one with whom she could leave the little ones when she went to work in the fields.

Regardless of what she felt, Assunta agreed to see Alessandro. She even paid for his trip, as Alessandro was too poor to pay his own way.

The meeting was set for Christmas Eve. The place was the rectory of St. Francis Church, where Assunta worked as a housekeeper.

As Alessandro faced Assunta for the first time in over thirty years, the tears streamed down his face and he knelt before her. "Assunta," he asked, "will you forgive me?"

Assunta too was in tears. "Maria has forgiven you," she said. "Must I not also forgive you?"

The parish priest invited Alessandro to stay for Christmas. "Assunta will cook one of her special dinners for us," he said. Alessandro hesitated.

"Yes, stay, Alessandro," Assunta insisted. Alessandro stayed and Assunta served him a delicious dinner. Later she mended his worn clothing.

That night, the people of the town gathered with special interest for the Christmas Midnight Mass. Word had gotten around that Alessandro Serenelli, Maria Goretti's murderer, had come to the rectory. As Assunta and Alessandro entered the Church and knelt side by side in the pew nearest to Maria's shrine, a deep hush fell over the assembly.

Maria, Santa!

On April 27, 1947, forty-five years after her death, Maria was beatified. A hundred thousand pilgrims filled St. Peter's Basilica, while another three hundred thousand gathered in the piazza outside. Assunta, now old and paralyzed, was wheeled into St. Peter's. At the sight of the mother, a great cheer broke from the thousands: "Viva la Mamma! Viva la Mamma!"

In his sermon, Cardinal Salotti said, "Without the teaching and example of her mother, Maria would never have been such a heroic girl. After God and her own brave heart, all the merit goes to her mother."

Assunta wept and said, "Dear Lord, I was not worthy of such an angel!"

Three years later, on June 24, 1950, Maria Goretti was canonized by Pope Pius XII. The ceremony was held outdoors, on the steps of St. Peter's, to accommodate the crowd of five hundred thousand pilgrims. In a wheelchair at the window of the Vatican, high above the throng, Assunta listened to the deafening cheers and wept again.

Meanwhile, in a quiet Capuchin monastery, a hired gardener tended his flowers. In his secret refuge, Alessandro too rejoiced.

Dear Maria,
There is someone
I want to forgive.
I am tired of carrying
this weight of anger.
But I am afraid to let go of it.
The anger has been a shield
protecting me from more hurt.
Without it I will be vulnerable again.
Pray for me
that I might have the courage
to lay down my anger.

5
Saint Rita of Cascia
Saint for Spouses of Alcoholics

On her wedding day every bride dreams that hers will be the perfect marriage. She imagines countless years of happiness enjoyed in the company of a loving, devoted husband who is conscious of her every need. She hopes to be blessed with beautiful, talented, respectful children whose achievements will make her proud. Alas, reality does not always equal one's dreams. Married life can bring many frustrations and sorrows, and leave many needs unmet.

The story of Saint Rita of Cascia shows that sanctity can grow even amid troubling, painful situations. Here is a woman who remained faithful to a difficult and abusive spouse, who raised two rebellious sons, who prayed while she cooked and cleaned the house, and who came to know the Lord's rewards toward the end of her seventy-six years on this earth.

Home life

Rita was born in 1381 in Roccaporena, Italy, to Antonio and Amata Mancini. An elderly peasant couple who had given up hope of having children, they showered their healthy daughter with an abundance of love and attention.

Though poor and illiterate, Antonio and Amata gave their daughter valuable personal lessons in the ways of Christian living. When a beggar would knock at the door of their home, he was always invited to come in. Amata would set a place for him at the family table and offer him lodging for the night. If there was work to be done, Antonio would invite the man to stay and help on the farm.

Moved by Jesus' gospel command to forgive and to love one's enemies, Antonio and Amata even went out of their way to care for the sick and wounded soldiers who frequently terrorized their village. Antonio personally took care of a crossbowman who had stolen and killed his most valuable farm animal — a strong ram.

Rita was inspired by her parents' faith and charity. In her teens, she felt that God wanted her to be a nun. One night after dinner, Rita kissed her parents and said plainly, "I have decided to become a nun."

Amata and Antonio were silent. Rita had expected to see joy and pride in their eyes; instead she saw pain and distress. "You are our only child," Amata said, "our solace and support." "We are advanced in years," Antonio added, "you cannot abandon us."

It was clear that Rita's parents could not accept her decision. She agreed to stay with them, consoling herself with a private thought: For the time being I will dedicate myself to God in the secret of my heart; later, I will enter the convent.

Marriage

Antonio and Amata had other plans for their only child. Overjoyed that Rita had given up the idea of entering a convent, Antonio quickly busied himself with finding a suitable son-in-law. "Rita will save the family from extinction," he said to Amata, "and a son-in-law will provide for us in our old age."

Imagine Rita's surprise when her father announced: "I have found a husband for you, Rita. Paolo Ferdinando has asked for your hand in marriage." Rita was shocked. Not only did she not want to marry, but her father's choice seemed unwise. Everyone in town knew that Paolo was a braggart, drank too much, and had a violent temper! Surely, Rita thought, God did not mean for her to marry Paolo.

Rita spoke boldly: "My parents, I do not wish any spouse but Jesus. To please you, I gave my promise not to enter a convent. I feel sure that without getting married I will still be able to console and comfort you and provide for all your necessities until God calls you to a happier home."

Her parents would not budge. "As a matter of fact," Antonio said, "I have already given my consent to Paolo. I cannot go back on my word."

Rita was left with no choice.

Paolo

At first, Paolo was good to Rita. He was a handsome man who could be quite charming and solicitous. He showered Rita with attention, curbed his drinking, controlled his temper, and stayed away from his rowdy gang. Rita was surprised and flattered by his efforts to turn over a new leaf. She grew to genuinely love him and was happy in her new way of life.

Rita's happiness was short-lived, however. Paolo soon slipped back into his old habits. He would spend long hours drinking at the town inn and come home sullen and unpredictable. He'd complain that Rita was spending too much on household expenses, then fly into a fit and smash any household object in reach. At other times he'd scream curses and threats at Rita, calm himself and apologize, then become enraged again and strike her.

Rita bore Paolo's abuse patiently. She refused to argue with him when he was drunk. Sometimes she answered him softly, trying to appease him. Other times she would not say a word. When he was done raging and roaring, she'd help him to bed.

Through it all she prayed and waited, hoping Paolo would come back to his senses.

Weeks turned into months. Paolo's rages grew more violent and noisy. Rita had to bear her neighbors' sympathy as well as Paolo's brutality. He openly paraded his unfaithfulness, staying away for nights at a time. Rita was determined not to indulge in self-pity. When neighbors would say how sorry they felt for her, she would answer cheerfully. "Paolo is not a bad man, and I do not regret having married him. I am confident that he will see the light and mend his ways."

Paolo's conversion

Antonio and Amata died shortly after Rita's marriage. They did not live to see their grandchildren, two spirited boys, born within a year of one another. Rita was comforted by the birth of her children. But she worried that they might be influenced by their father.

As the boys entered their teens, Rita's fears were confirmed. The same scowl that was always on Paolo's face appeared on the faces of her children. They began testing their mother and rebelling. Rita's patience was nearly spent.

One evening, after being away for a whole day and night, Paolo returned home with his clothing torn and his face scarred. He had been in a fight and was more irritable than usual. Rita stood by the fire, stirring the soup. Paolo came up behind her and demanded to know why his supper was not ready. Rita's eyes flashed with indignation, but she did not answer. Paolo became furious and slapped her.

Rita turned on her heel, left the house, and went out to the garden. She hesitated, perhaps saying a prayer, before reentering the house. Then, with unprecedented candor, Rita vented her anger. She told Paolo exactly what she thought of his childish behavior. She did not wait for a response. Expecting a violent rebuke, Rita fled to her room and locked the door.

All was quiet. Rita waited nervously, wondering why Paolo did not curse and beat on the door. She had never before spoken angrily to him. When she finally dared to draw the bolt and look out, she saw Paolo sitting at the dinner table with his head bowed. She approached him timidly and took his hand in hers. His hand trembled and he began to weep.

"Forgive me, Rita," he stammered. "I am unworthy of you." Rita was stunned.

A triumph of grace

A difficult struggle began after Paolo's initial repentance. While Paolo had recognized and confessed his weaknesses to Rita and to God, it was not easy to change his lifelong habits. He needed a new self-image and a strong will. He still sometimes came home drunk, but Rita no longer feared him. If the old violence began to rise in him, Paolo would rush madly off to the forest and not return until he'd regained his self-control.

When his temptations seemed overwhelming, Paolo depended on Rita's encouragement. "When an unwelcome visitor knocks at your door and you do not answer," she said, "he will keep up his efforts for quite a long time. When he sees they are in vain, he will go away and leave you at peace. Remember, Paolo, God himself is helping you."

At times Paolo despaired and said to Rita, "I am lost. There can be no salvation for me; I have too greatly offended the Lord for him to ever pardon me." Rita would then rebuke him with strong words, "You insult your loving Father. There is no greater sin than to refuse his mercy. This is more offensive to him than all the sins you have committed in the past."

More trials

It would be nice to report that Rita and Paolo lived happily ever after. But Paolo had made many enemies before he repented and reformed. One evening, on his way home from business in Cascia, he was savagely murdered. A neighbor was sent to Rita's house to tell her and the boys. As the neighbor haltingly delivered the message, Rita cried out in anguish. The boys, now nearly twenty years of age, rose angrily to their feet and said, "God hear our vow! We will avenge our father!"

The family went out to the square where villagers were gathering with torches. Together they walked on the path to Cascia until they came to the place where Paolo's body lay. As she walked, Rita murmured, "He is no more, he is no more." Before his mutilated body she knelt down and said, "May God pardon the murderers as I have forgiven them."

Rita's expression of forgiveness had no effect on her sons. Revenge was the law of the mountains. It terrified Rita to overhear her sons' murderous plans. She tried to reason with them, but they withdrew from her. With despair Rita watched her sons grow bitter and quarrelsome, then turn to drink as their father had once done. When they announced that they had found out who had murdered their father, and when they had planned their attack, Rita's prayers to God became desperate.

"O my God," Rita prayed, "take the life of my children if it is necessary, but save them from sin and eternal damnation!" It was a cruel mercy Rita asked for, but she feared bodily death less than spiritual death. God apparently honored her prayer. Before they could carry out their vengeful mission, Rita's sons became ill and died.

Convent

The months following the death of her husband and sons passed slowly. Rita, not quite forty years old and already alone in the world, once again considered religious life. One morning, after giving away all her belongings, Rita set out for the Augustinian convent in Cascia. When she reached the place on the path where Paolo had been murdered, Rita fell to the ground, weeping. She was filled with confusion and anguish over the death of her husband and sons. It was with great difficulty that she rose and continued on the path to Cascia, arriving after nightfall.

Imagine Rita's distress when she knocked at the door of the convent and was refused admittance with a crisp, "I'm sorry, but the rule permits only virgins. There are no exceptions." She stayed the night and then was sent back to Roccaporena.

A second time Rita approached the prioress. Again she was refused admittance. But Rita lacked neither patience nor perseverance. The third time she approached the prioress, Rita was accepted into the Augustinians.

Rita's life in community was unspectacular for the most part. She was respected and loved by her community. She prayed and worked with the joy of one who has waited a long time for the fulfillment of a dream. Like everyone else, she struggled with temptations and doubts. There was, however, one very special event in Rita's religious life.

Rita prayed unceasingly that she might be privileged to share deeply in Christ's sufferings. One day, as she knelt at the foot of the crucifix in the chapel, weeping with sorrow for her sins, a thorn wound appeared on her forehead. It was extremely painful and caused her to faint. The Sisters helped her to her room but the wound gave out such a strong, fetid odor that Rita was reassigned to a corner cell in the convent. For the final years of her life she bore this humiliation and suffering joyfully, counting it a blessing of the crucified Christ.

Death

Rita died on May 22, 1457. One biographer says that the instant she died, the convent bell rang out three times, though no one had touched it. A wonderful fragrance filled the convent, and the wound on Rita's forehead was completely healed. Her body remains incorrupt to this day.

Rita was canonized on May 24, 1900, by Pope Leo XIII. Many miracles, from the raising of a dead child to astonishing conversions, have been attributed to her intercession. She is appropriately designated as the saint of impossible and desperate cases.

Dear Rita,
It's so easy these days
to give up on marriage.
We think we've won
if we just stick it out,
stay reasonably faithful,
and don't get a divorce.
I don't want my marriage to be mediocre.
I want to cherish my spouse
the way Christ cherishes his Church.
Please pray for me, Rita.

6
Blessed Maria Bagnesi
Saint for the Sick

Maria Bagnesi knew the torments of both mental and physical illness. Her physical health was irreversibly damaged in infancy. She had been inadequately fed by a wet nurse as a baby and never quite recovered. As a young woman she had a nervous breakdown which left her a bedridden invalid for long periods throughout the rest of her life. As an adult she suffered from asthma, kidney troubles, digestive troubles, and frequent fevers.

Even greater than Maria's pain, however, was her love for God. Despite her physical and mental ailments, Maria loved God and believed that he loved her. "I know that I am sick, but I will still bless the Lord," she said. "He wills me to follow him lying down."

The sick and troubled came to Maria's bedside, and from the depths of her darkness she reached out to them. She was graced with an extraordinary compassion born of her own suffering. Through her guidance and prayers enemies were reconciled, sinners were converted, and the troubled were consoled.

Early life

Maria Bagnesi was born on August 24, 1514, in Florence, Italy. Her parents, Carlo Rineri Bagnesi and his wife Alexandra, were members of the nobility. They entrusted their baby daughter to a wet nurse, as was customary in those days. But the wet nurse had no milk. Apparently Carlo and Alexandra did not know this and the nurse did not tell them. Maria would have starved to death if it were not for the kindness of some neighbors who gave the nurse a sheep. The nurse began to feed Maria sheep's milk, but Maria's stomach suffered permanent damage.

Despite her physical sufferings, Maria was pretty and intelligent. Being the baby of the family, she was doted on by her parents and two older sisters. As a young girl, she often visited one of her older sisters at the convent where she was a nun. This sister, to amuse the other nuns, would ask little Maria, "Who will you marry?" Maria would respond, "I love Jesus. He will be my husband."

Maria truly seemed to have a special, childlike love for God. One day her mother said that she was going to church the next morning to hear a homily. Maria asked excitedly if she could go too. Her mother thought Maria would forget about it by morning, so she said, "OK. I'll call you in the morning." When her mother awoke early the next day, she was surprised to find Maria dressed and ready to go. Maria had slept fitfully and awakened before dawn, so eager was she to go to church.

When Maria was in her early teens, her mother's health began to decline. She was left to run the house and to care for her mother by herself. Maria did not allow these responsibilities to impinge upon her prayer life. She said, "Without prayer I am a fish out of water."

Her mother, Alexandra, died when Maria was about seventeen. Her father, Carlo, called her aside then and asked her if she would like to be a religious or to remain in the world. Maria was unexpectedly overcome with fear and could not answer her father. It is not clear in the biography written by her confessor, Father Alexander Copoccium, why her father's question caused such an unusual response. Perhaps the question came at a bad time, so soon after her mother's death. Whatever the reason, the shock was so great that Maria suffered a nervous breakdown.

Maria was confined to her bed, "filled from head to toe with torments," writes her biographer. Carlo anxiously called in the best doctors and a variety of self-proclaimed healers. Of course the science of psychiatry was non-existent in Maria's time, and the practice of medicine was in a rather primitive state. The doctors shook their heads and prescribed bedrest. The "healers" brought useless homemade concoctions: a chicken mixture of some sort, oily syrups, a body plaster made of salt, pepper, and many other ingredients. Rather than help Maria, the plaster treatment nearly caused her death. It burned her skin and caused her such severe pain that she became comatose for a time.

Dominican tertiary

After this frustrating series of treatments, Maria assured her father that she would live without the help of doctors or healers. "I have faith in God, and I commend myself to him," she said. A peaceful period followed. Maria saw to the erection of a little altar in her room and filled her days with prayer. Carlo was afraid that she would not live long. He knew Maria wanted to be a Dominican nun, so he contacted the friars and told them of his daughter's desire. A Dominican priest named Father Vector came to see Maria. He spoke with her and gave her Communion, then he blessed a habit and placed it on her shoulders. Father Vector explained to Maria the responsibilities that came with the habit, but gently advised her to keep a minimal prayer schedule so as not to further endanger her health.

At the age of thirty-two, Maria took the vows of a Dominican Tertiary in Father Vector's presence. "My Jesus," she said, "I cannot thank you enough for inspiring me with the desire to enter this state. Give me the grace to be faithful to it."

Soon after her profession, Maria's health improved dramatically. Maria joyfully received this as a "marriage gift" from God. She was able to attend church and to visit her sisters at the convents where they lived. Many people in the city who knew of Maria's chronic illness were amazed at her sudden cure. They marveled at her recovery and began to talk among themselves about this wondrous event.

Unfortunately, Maria's cure was short-lived. Before long she was back in her bed with pneumonia, kidney troubles, high fevers, and insomnia. She was apparently tormented by a fear of the dark, and could not be left without light day and night. The doctors turned away her visitors for a while to allow her some peace and quiet.

Charity

Although Maria did not invite attention, the people of Florence soon decided that she was worth praising and seeking out. They sensed there was something special about Maria — a closeness to God despite, or even because of, her sufferings. People with troubles began coming to the door of the Bagnesi house asking to see her. When one of Maria's doctors finally agreed to admit a visitor to her room, Maria appeared to revive completely. He was amazed, and began to allow more visitors.

One woman came to Maria's bed filled with anger and bitterness toward a man who had hurt her. Maria spoke gently with her, advising her to forgive the offender. The woman exploded and said, "What? Should I condone the injury? If I could I would rip out his heart and chew it up!" Maria tried to calm her, but her words only got the woman more wrought up. Finally, Maria got out of her bed, knelt at the feet of the woman, and asked her pardon. This simple, humble act softened the woman's heart.

Innocent and fragile though Maria was, she was not scandalized by other's sins or intimidated by evil people. Her biographer says, "Men who were callous sinners would be converted in her presence and would rather die than sin again." On one occasion a particularly dangerous-looking man was escorted into Maria's room. Maria sat up in bed when he entered the room. She began to speak, but the man interrupted and said that he would like to see her alone. Maria nodded and signaled the escort to leave the room. After the escort had left, Maria turned to the man and told him that he was right in requesting that the escort leave. "He may have been killed if he had stayed," she said. An exorcism followed. When the escort returned the man was at peace and laughing.

Maria was increasingly preoccupied with the needs of others. From her bed she begged people to help various individuals and groups. She asked visitors to donate money for the upkeep of a monastery, or for the dowry of an unwed girl, or for clothes for the poor.

Maria's prayer life was her bridge to others and to the outside world. She prayed for the city of Florence, in danger of a damaging flood. She prayed for two students who were bitter enemies and in danger of killing one another: They later became friends and credited their reconciliation to Maria's prayers.

Maria prayed for a young man awaiting execution. Though he was not at fault, he had been condemned to death for gravely injuring another person in a fight. A relative of the young man came to see Maria and explained the situation to her. Maria calmly assured the relative, "Trust in God, and he will be freed." Two weeks later the sentence was suddenly waived and the young man was released.

Maria's spiritual life was rich with prophetic dreams, visions, and ecstacies. But she did not like to call attention to these special experiences. She tried, in fact, to make light of them and cover them up. A friend of hers said, "If you did not know Maria well she would appear very ordinary. We who speak to her intimately, however, know the great depth of her interior life. In seeing this, we praise God for giving us someone like Maria and for manifesting his love through her life."

Trials and death

Not everything was sweetness and light for Maria. "Look how the devil tempts me," Maria said. "He tries to tell me that my evil is nothing more than a figment of my imagination. Then he calls me a hypocrite, and says that I am only pretending to be good. These are more painful than my other sufferings." When her spiritual director told her to disregard the accusations of the devil, she answered, "I know that I should not believe these things, but they do bother me."

Some people distrusted Maria. A priest came to visit Maria, secretly determined to find out if she was demonically possessed. He hid some relics in his clothing, thinking that if she were possessed she would react with fear or anger to the holy objects. To the contrary, his conversation with Maria so moved and encouraged him that he left convinced of her holiness.

As Maria aged, her physical health quickly deteriorated. There was a period when she lost her sight and hearing. She was overcome with weariness and a desire to die. "Lord, I do not want to insult you," she prayed, "but what good is this body of mine? I would gladly die, yet I know that it is your will that no one harm herself."

Maria's final illness began with a creeping paralysis. It originated in her legs and gradually rose through her body until she could not even swallow the Host in Communion. She died in 1577 at the age of sixty-three. Her confessor and a friend were present to anoint her and pray with her. Just before she died she raised her head a bit and opened her eyes. Her expression was such that those present felt sure she saw angels waiting to take her to heaven.

"If I were asked to give someone advice," Maria once said, "I would say to . . . have a great devotion to Mary, take good care of your time, do not allow occasions for doing good to pass. Don't be solicitious that the world know you; for the person will be blessed who cares nothing about the affairs of the world. The person who does these things will have peace and quiet."

Though confined to one small room for much of her adult life, Maria Bagnesi had a sense of love that did not keep her enclosed in herself. She cared deeply about others and the problems of the outside world. While her body withered, her spirit soared and extended itself to embrace the world.

> *Dear Maria,*
> *There is pain*
> *and there is darkness*
> *that will not leave me.*
> *I pray, but I do not improve.*
> *I do not want to lose hope of healing;*
> *but if healing is not to be my answer,*
> *I do not want to lose faith and love.*
> *Please, Maria,*
> *help me to see past my own suffering*
> *to the suffering and needs of others.*

7
Saint Hyacintha Mariscotti
The Accidental Nun

It's well and good when a young woman decides to be a nun and joyfully chooses a life of poverty, celibacy, and obedience. But how about the woman who is unhappily forced to live one of these "religious" virtues? Poverty is painful when you are the wife of an unemployed spouse, barely scraping together enough money to feed and clothe your family. Obedience is obnoxious for the employee with a brute for a boss. Celibacy or complete chastity is difficult for the young woman whose deepest desire is to marry, but who cannot find a suitable spouse.

Saint Hyacintha was a nun without a religious vocation. She had wanted to marry, but since no one asked for her hand in marriage she was forced to enter the convent. She did not want to be the spouse of Christ. She balked at the idea of obedience. She could not imagine life without the seventeenth-century equivalent of diamonds and designer dresses. For years Hyacintha holed up in an elegantly furnished convent suite, filing her fingernails and cursing her fate. It was a bitter, lonely life.

This is the story of Hyacintha's struggle to make peace with her life.

Early life

Hyacintha was born in 1585 in Vignanello, Italy. She was the second of three daughters born to Count Marc-Antonio di Mariscotti and Ottavia Orsini. Her parents were wealthy, distinguished Catholics. In regal fashion she was baptized by the Bishop of the city-state of Castellana.

In her teens, Hyacintha was sent to a convent school run by the Third Order Franciscan nuns. Her elder sister, Innocentia, was already a Franciscan nun. But Hyacintha did not take well to convent rules. She was interested in boys, clothes, and having fun — not in prayers and good works. The nuns sent her back to the castle.

Back home, Hyacintha fell in love. A certain dashing nobleman began making frequent visits to the castle. Hyacintha dressed carefully, daydreamed, and blushed appealingly whenever he was near. The nobleman was rich and well-bred. Hyacintha could almost hear her family congratulating her. "A brilliant marriage!" they would say. Everyone would be pleased.

But Hyacintha's dreams turned bitter the day the young nobleman came to the castle and asked not for her, but for her little sister Ortensia. Hyacintha was stunned and heartbroken. How could he? How could *she*? Hyacintha was consumed with anger and jealousy.

The nobleman soon asked for Ortensia's hand in marriage, and the Mariscottis gave their consent. Hyacintha was left to nurse not only her broken heart, but her bruised pride as well. In those days, it was very unusual for a younger sister to be given in marriage before the elder sister. Hyacintha was humiliated. She could hardly bear the pitying glances of her relatives and the whispered talk behind her back. She kept her spirits up with the thought that there were plenty of eligible men in Italy. A beautiful young woman from a good family would not have to wait long for another suitor.

Hyacintha waited. And waited. But no suitor came.

Convent

Hyacintha became moody and ill-humored as the years passed. When she was twenty years old — long past the usual marriageable age at that time — her parents urged her to enter the convent. Hyacintha agreed to go, seeing that she had no better choice. Her father breathed a sigh of relief and gave Hyacintha a magnificent going away party.

The Franciscan nuns, however, could hardly be expected to cheer when they learned that Hyacintha was to rejoin them. Her previous stay with them had been difficult, to say the least. Despite their hesitations, the nuns were not about to endanger the relationship with their generous patron, Count di Mariscotti. They received Hyacintha graciously and prayed that religious life would change her for the better.

Hyacintha had her own ideas about religious life and quickly announced them. "Though I wear the habit of a nun I intend to claim every indulgence possible for myself in virture of my rank and the wealth of my family."

Hyacintha's "habit" was an elegant gown of velvet and silk. She selected several rooms of the convent and had them beautifully furnished at her father's expense. She insisted on keeping her own cook and eating alone in her quarters. The years passed slowly as the nuns tolerated Hyacintha and Hyacintha tolerated the nuns.

At the age of thirty, Hyacintha became ill. She was plagued with severe headaches, fatigue, depression, and digestive troubles. Since she was unable to go to her confessor — a poor Franciscan priest — he came to see her. When he saw the luxury surrounding Hyacintha, he was shocked and said he could not hear her confession until she changed her ways. He told Hyacintha that he was scandalized by her lifestyle and afraid to imagine what this revealed about her spiritual condition.

Hyacintha burst into tears. "Father, is there no remedy for me?" she asked. "Have I shut myself up in the cloister only to lose my soul?" The priest answered her gently. He assured her that everything would be all right if she would change her ways. He told her that as soon as she was well, she should put on a simple habit and make a public confession to the community.

Hyacintha did as she was told, begging forgiveness of her fellow sisters. Despite this show of repentance, she was not yet ready to give up her splendid rooms, her personal cook, or her independence. For a short time she made small sacrifices and became more involved in the community's spiritual exercises. Hyacintha had spent many years doing things her way, however, and she did not find it easy to change. Gradually she slipped back into her old lifestyle and her self-centered ways. Again she became ill and miserable.

To know love

Utterly exhausted and depressed, Hyacintha looked up from her sickbed at a statue of Catherine of Siena. She noticed the inscription beneath it which read, "What do I wish for, Lord, or what could I wish for, outside of Thee?" Hyacintha was overcome with longing. She suddenly wanted more than anything in the world to know the love that Saint Catherine had known. She prayed to Saint Catherine, begging the great fourteenth-century saint to take her to this God who would fill and heal her heart. She gained courage as she felt she heard Catherine saying, "Enter bravely upon this way; I will be your advocate, and will protect you always."

Hyacintha was elated. Saint Catherine cared! Saint Catherine would be her friend and helper! Hyacintha wanted to bound out of her bed, she was so happy. Her health soon improved. She gave away all of her beautiful furnishings and comforts. She took off her elegant gown and put on the ragged habit that had been left behind by a deceased nun. She discharged her personal cook and asked to be given only the simplest foods.

The change in Hyacintha's attitude and actions was extreme.

She had an enormous amount of pent-up energy after so many years of luxury and bedrest. She began an ambitious schedule of prayer, penances, and charitable works. She was by no means a sober and long-faced saint. Her biographers give a picture of a lively, witty woman with a keen awareness of both her weaknesses and strengths.

"She had no lack of temptations," writes a biographer. "She was tempted against faith: to believe that God did not, after all, exist; for which temptation flowers and birds were her medicine. She was tempted with the idea that heaven would be boring. To this fear she made answer with sardonic logic: 'Well, the only alternative is hell!' "

She was afraid she would not find love in heaven. Saint Catherine consoled her with the message: "You will come to the holy love of God." Hyacintha was so insecure, however, that she could not make herself believe Saint Catherine's words and pleaded for a sign. "As a sign, make a certain individual bring me a rose," Hyacintha thought. It just so happened that the individual found a beautiful rose growing in his garden, out of season. He decided to give it to the bishop, but at the door to the bishop's residence he suddenly changed his mind and brought it to Sister Hyacintha instead. When Hyacintha saw the rose she leapt for joy and skipped around the room in circles singing, "I *shall* come to true love! I *shall* come to true love!"

Because of her melancholy temperament, Hyacintha feared solitude. She would sometimes panic when she was alone in her tiny cell. She would go outside to breathe a little, but return again to her cell with a wry smile and say, "If I die of it, patience! Die then!"

Charitable works

After her personal reform, Hyacintha's strengths showed through. She was wonderfully compassionate and wise in counselling others. The people of the city of Viterbo trusted and respected Hyacintha; they confessed their darkest secrets to the beloved Sister. Hyacintha said, "The sort of people who most appeal to me are those who are despised, who are devoid of self-love, and who have little sensible consolation."

After a time, Hyacintha was appointed mistress of novices. Several biographers note that she was uncommonly gifted in this role, guiding her admiring young charges with skill and gentleness.

Hyacintha nursed the sick during an epidemic and was deeply moved by the suffering she saw. She later founded two confraternities: one for collecting alms for the sick, the poor, and prisoners; the other for finding homes for the aged. "Why cannot I change myself into bread and clothing to give to the poor?" she said. "Why will not my heart multiply itself so that I can cover them all with love?"

Hyacintha loved the Blessed Mother so much that she would light up whenever she heard a neighbor calling to someone named Maria. She signed her name "Hyacintha di Maria," and loved to have any item set aside for her use to be labeled "For Maria."

Hyacintha's desire for others to know God's love burned in her like a fever. "O My God," she would cry, "why can I not go out into the streets and public places? I would cry out with all my strength. Is it possible to be so senseless as not to realize that this world is nothing and you are everything? O my God! Unknown God! Is it possible that men can care more for this earth than for you, true treasure and only good?"

Having once experienced the Lord's love, Hyacintha could hardly contain her joy. She had found the passionate love of God, and her starved heart was filled at last. She would never again curse the fate that had driven her into God's arms.

Death

Hyacintha died on January 30, 1640, at the age of fifty-five. She was prepared to go to God, having said serenely that morning, "I am going to my own country this evening." After her death, her skin became white and ruddy, and her body gave off an enchanting scent. Many miracles occurred at her grave. She was canonized by Pope Pius VII in 1807. Her feast is kept by all branches of the Franciscan Order.

Hyacintha's story echoes the Serenity Prayer, "God, grant me the serenity to accept the things I cannot change, the courage to change the things I can, and the wisdom to know the difference." Hyacintha found peace and fulfillment when she accepted the life she could not change. She blossomed late, but beautifully.

Dear Hyacintha,
It is hard to know
when to let go of dreams.
It is hard to trust God
when his will threatens to contradict
my desires.
Hyacintha, please help me keep God
first in my life.
Help me believe his promise:
"Take delight in the Lord
and he will give you
the desires of your heart."

Saints for Today and Tomorrow

In a bygone era noted for its precision and legalism, one pope decreed that Catholics should call no one a saint unless he or she had been so declared by the Church. Nevertheless, this statement did not stop the use of the word "saint" to refer to the holy people of the early Church whose saintliness was recognized without a formal inquiry into their virtuous lives. In this manuscript the word "saint" has been used to refer to all seven holy women when in reality only five are canonized saints; the other two have simply been declared "blessed."

Today the legalism of using the word "saint" only for officially canonized saints tends to be overlooked. Many Catholics seem willing to forego the formal procedure in favor of honestly assessing the lives of exemplary contemporaries and then, if they are judged worthy, of pronouncing them "living saints."

Such a practice may not be all bad! Observing those special people who embody the presence of God as Jesus did, we can recognize holiness in action. Seeing lives of dedicated service, admiring people of deep prayerfulness, and noting individuals who model the essence of Christianity in their every action can be an inspiration to us. There might really be some saints in our midst.

Women like the late Dorothy Day, the foundress of the Catholic Worker Movement, and Mother Teresa of Calcutta, recognized internationally for her work with the poor, are regularly declared to be "saintly women." There are others like them whose lives have been scrutinized and publicized by the media coverage they receive. Their virtues have been tested by the passage of time. The temptation to place fame and glory ahead of continued service to God's people has not won them over. They have been found worthy of popular acclaim as "saints for today."

It is quite likely that there are other equally holy women who go undiscovered by television and newspapers. While lacking international acclaim, their holiness of life is clear to the relatives, neighbors, and fellow parishioners who know them and who are blessed by their presence. These are women who are exposed to the same problems, difficulties, and temptations as their counterparts across the country and throughout the world. Seeing them succeed at living the Christian life in a saintly way can be as inspiring as watching a news report about Mother Teresa or reading the life of a saint from another century.

While saintliness can seem mystifying and mystical, it can also be quite ordinary and quite attainable. The purpose of this book has been to enable people to learn about saints who suffered rather ordinary, everyday trials but who triumphed over them. In the midst of their ordinary lives, these women found the key to saintliness. They lived the Gospel message extraordinarily well.

The readers of these pages are offered a challenge: Absorb the lessons of these holy women and become the saints of tomorrow by living ordinary lives in the best way possible.

(At the request of the author, these concluding thoughts were written by Rev. Thomas R. Artz, C.SS.R., managing editor, Book and Pamphlet Department, Liguori Publications.)

MORE BOOKS FOR WOMEN

WOMAN AT MIDLIFE
Moving Beyond Stereotypes
by Vernie Dale

Focusing on both the psychological and spiritual needs of today's woman, this book presents a positive approach to a sometimes bewildering and difficult time. It helps women see the mid-life passage as a time of opportunity — a time to turn from chaos to Christian joy and from fear to fulfillment. **$2.95**

TO LOVE AND TO BE LOVED
Secrets of Intimacy
by John C. Tormey

Going beyond commercialized concepts of "love," this book speaks of true "intimacy" — something that can only be achieved through patience, prudence, and the inconvenience of really caring. A book for any couple who seeks to deepen the Christian commitment of a truly intimate relationship. **$1.95**

FROM VICTIM TO DECISION-MAKER
by Marilyn Norquist Gustin

Presents a joyful vision of our own power of choice — and how we can use this power to turn unchosen circumstances into self-affirming, faith-affirming experiences. With compassion and understanding, this book shows how even the most painful situations can be remedied by a change in attitude. Includes points for reflection and suggests helpful Scripture readings. **$1.50**

THE SINGLE LIFE
A Christian Challenge
by Martha M. Niemann

A book for those faced with the ups and downs, joys and sorrows, hopes and frustrations of being a single Christian adult. Thirty brief chapters explore the unique problems and situations of single life and help readers discover the roads to happiness as single Christians. **$4.25**

INNER CALM
A Christian Answer to Modern Stress
by Dr. Paul DeBlassie III

Combines modern psychology with spirituality to help readers discover greater peace and joy through the centuries-old method of meditation known as the "Jesus Prayer." Contains a wealth of healing experiences and offers a way to find true inner calm in today's world. **$3.95**

Order from your local bookstore or write to:
Liguori Publications, Box 060, Liguori, Missouri 63057
*(Please add 75¢ for postage and handling for
first item ordered and 25¢ for each additional item.)*